D1733189

BREEDS

German Shepherds

by Mari Schuh

Consultant:
Michael Leuthner, D.V.M.
PetCare Clinic, Madison, Wisc.

BLASTOFF!
4
READERS

BELLWETHER MEDIA · MINNEAPOLIS, MN

Note to Librarians, Teachers, and Parents:

Blastoff! Readers are carefully developed by literacy experts and combine standards-based content with developmentally appropriate text.

Level 1 provides the most support through repetition of high-frequency words, light text, predictable sentence patterns, and strong visual support.

Level 2 offers early readers a bit more challenge through varied simple sentences, increased text load, and less repetition of high-frequency words.

Level 3 advances early-fluent readers toward fluency through increased text and concept load, less reliance on visuals, longer sentences, and more literary language.

Level 4 builds reading stamina by providing more text per page, increased use of punctuation, greater variation in sentence patterns, and increasingly challenging vocabulary.

Level 5 encourages children to move from "learning to read" to "reading to learn" by providing even more text, varied writing styles, and less familiar topics.

Whichever book is right for your reader, Blastoff! Readers are the perfect books to build confidence and encourage a love of reading that will last a lifetime!

This edition first published in 2009 by Bellwether Media.

No part of this publication may be reproduced in whole or in part without written permission of the publisher. For information regarding permission, write to Bellwether Media Inc., Attention: Permissions Department, Post Office Box 19349, Minneapolis, MN 55419-0349.

Library of Congress Cataloging-in-Publication Data
Schuh, Mari C., 1975-
  German shepherds / by Mari Schuh.
    p. cm. — (Blastoff! readers. Dog breeds)
  Includes bibliographical references and index.
  Summary: "Simple text and full color photographs introduce beginning readers to the characteristics of the dog breed German Shepherds. Developed by literacy experts for students in kindergarten through third grade"—Provided by publisher.
  ISBN-13: 978-1-60014-215-4 (hardcover : alk. paper)
  ISBN-10: 1-60014-215-X (hardcover : alk. paper)
  1. German shepherd dog—Juvenile literature. I. Title.

SF429.G37S38 2008
636.737'6—dc22
                                                    2008019999

Contents

What Are German Shepherds?

German Shepherd Dogs are smart and energetic dogs. German Shepherds, as they are commonly called, are very **loyal** and famous for their courage.

German Shepherds were first used as **herding** dogs. Today, this **breed** can do many jobs.

German Shepherds are strong and muscular. They are medium-sized and have long bodies, pointed ears, and long, bushy tails.

! fun fact

In the British Isles, German Shepherds are also known as Alsatians.

Most adult German Shepherds weigh
75 to 85 pounds (34 to 38.5 kilograms)
and are 22 to 26 inches (56 to 66
centimeters) tall at the shoulder.

German Shepherds have two **coats**, an inner coat and an outer coat. Together, these coats protect the dogs from wind, rain, snow, and freezing temperatures.

Most German Shepherds have black and tan coats. They can also be black and gray, all white, or all black. Some German Shepherds have hints of blue, silver, or red in their coat.

History of German Shepherds

People have used German Shepherds to herd and guard sheep for hundreds of years. People would take two of the best herding German Shepherds and let them have puppies. Their puppies were even better herding dogs.

! fun fact

Rin Tin Tin was a famous German Shepherd that appeared in 26 movies in the 1920s and 1930s.

The history of German Shepherds started with a man named Max von Stephanitz. Max wanted a great herding dog. In 1899, Max bought a dog at a **dog show**.

Max named the dog Horand.
Horand was very loyal to Max.
Horand was lively and smart.
Max started to train Horand.
Horand quickly learned
new skills.

Max von Stephanitz

Horand had good manners. He behaved well around people. Horand was also a good guard dog.

Max decided he wanted more dogs like Horand. Horand and a female dog had puppies. Max called the dogs and their puppies German Shepherds. Horand became the very first German Shepherd.

In 1899, Max created the first dog club for German Shepherds. Horand was the first member. The dog club set up rules for how German Shepherds should look and behave.

German Shepherds Today

German Shepherds have a powerful sense of smell. They are **alert** and easy to train. These traits make them great **working dogs**. They can do many jobs.

German Shepherds work with disabled people and sick people. They guide people who are blind. Some dogs also spend time with sick people in hospitals. This helps cheer up the sick people.

German Shepherds also work with the police and the military. Their sharp sense of smell makes them great at finding bombs, illegal drugs, and lost people. The police and military use German Shepherds as guard dogs.

Special police and military units called **K-9s** pair an officer with a dog. German Shepherds are often used in this role because of their skills and intelligence.

19

German Shepherds need to spend lots of time with people. They need to be kept busy with work. If the dogs don't have anything to do, they become unhappy and could cause trouble.

German Shepherds are hardworking dogs that enjoy a challenge. They can be great workers, helpers, and friends.

Glossary

alert—paying attention to what is happening and being ready for action

breed—a type of dog

coat—the hair or fur of an animal

dog show—a competitive event where dogs are judged

herding—making people or animals move as a group

K-9s—police and military units that pair an officer with a dog

loyal—faithful; German Shepherds are loyal to their owners.

working dog—a breed of dog that does jobs to help people

To Learn More

AT THE LIBRARY
Fiedler, Julie. *German Shepherd Dogs*. New York:
PowerKids Press, 2006.

Gray, Susan Heinrichs. *German Shepherds*.
Mankato, Minn.: Child's World, 2008.

Stone, Lynn M. *German Shepherds*. Vero Beach,
Fla.: Rourke, 2003.

ON THE WEB
Learning more about
German Shepherds
is as easy as 1, 2, 3.

1. Go to www.factsurfer.com

2. Enter "German Shepherds" into search box.

3. Click the "Surf" button and you will see a list of
   related web sites.

With factsurfer.com, finding more information is just a
click away.

Index

The images in this book are reproduced through the courtesy of: Kevin Russ, front cover; Mark Raycroft / Getty Images, pp. 4, 6, 7, 8, 14, 21; Petra Wegner / Alamy, pp. 5, 9, 20; Pix 'n Pages, pp. 9, 16; mediacolor's / Alamy, p. 11; Monika Wisniewska, pp.12-13; MaxVonStephanitz, p. 13 (inset); JUNIORS BILDARCHIV / agefotostock, p. 17; blickwinkel / Alamy, p. 18; KonradZelazowski / Alamy, p. 19.

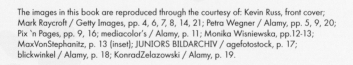